The Dragon in the Drawer

A graphic novel

Story by Cameron Macintosh

Illustrations by Irma Ruggiero

The Dragon in the Drawer

Text: Cameron Macintosh
Publishers: Tania Mazzeo and Eliza Webb
Series consultant: Amanda Sutera
  Hands on Heads Consulting
Editor: Sarah Layton
Project editor: Annabel Smith
Designer: Jess Kelly
Project designer: Danielle Maccarone
Illustrations: Irma Ruggiero
Production controller: Renee Tome

NovaStar

Cengage Learning Australia
Level 5, 80 Dorcas Street
Southbank VIC 3006 Australia
Phone: 1300 790 853
Email: aust.nelsonprimary@cengage.com

For learning solutions, visit **cengage.com.au**

Printed in China by 1010 Printing International Ltd
1 2 3 4 5 6 7 28 27 26 25 24

*Nelson acknowledges the Traditional Owners and Custodians
of the lands of all First Nations Peoples. We pay respect
to Elders past and present, and extend that respect to
all First Nations Peoples today.*

Contents

Chapter 1

After the Storm

Early in the year 1627, a wild storm struck the town of Loreville.

Otis and his older sister, Janaya, were lying in their beds, anxiously listening to the thunder.

Their parents were asleep in the next room.

The next morning ...

Otis, look! There's something on top of the chimney!

I'll go up and see what it is.

What is it?

I don't know! I'll bring it down so you can have a look.

What do you think it could be?

5

I think it's some kind of gigantic egg. And the only creature big enough to lay an egg this size is the dragon that lives up on Hawker's Hill.

This egg needs to be far from here when it hatches! We have to tell Mum and Dad.

But Mum and Dad will talk to the other townsfolk and the egg will be taken away. That wouldn't be fair – the dragon on Hawker's Hill has never hurt anyone.

Dragons aren't all dangerous. Remember what the dragon in the forest did when those wolves followed me?

The dragon scared the wolves away and saved my life.

You're right, Otis. Dragons aren't all bad. Let's return this egg to its mother.

Chapter 2

An Unhappy Dragon

12

She didn't see the egg. What do we do now?

We'll just have to bring it back inside and think of another plan.

13

Chapter 3
The Baby in the Drawer

Wow, it really loves bread!

Just then, Otis and Janaya heard their mum and dad talking.

They say the dragon's rebuilt her nest.

Don't worry. Me and some other townsfolk are going to trap her if she comes back to town.

Chapter 4

Back to the Nest

Later that day ...

There's the dragon in her new nest!

I see her too! It's just as well dragons sleep during the daytime!

There's smoke coming out of her nose! That means she'll be awake soon.

I know, but ... we have to stick to our plan.

This is as close as we can go. But we can use this rope to help send the baby up to her.

Okay, I hope your bow and arrow does the trick!

Janaya and Otis pulled the baby dragon along the rope, up towards the nest.

Let's take it slowly.

Yes! If the mother wakes, we don't know what she might do!

Otis and Janaya returned home. Now they could tell the town they were safe.

I told you dragons aren't all bad!

The dragon and her baby were now safe, too.

The End